Lucca
Travel Guide

Quick Trips Series

No part of this publication may be reproduced, stored in a retrieval system, or transmitted, in any form or by any means without the prior written permission of the publisher, nor be otherwise circulated in any form of binding or cover other than that in which it is published and without similar condition being imposed on the subsequent purchaser. If there are any errors or omissions in copyright acknowledgements the publisher will be pleased to insert the appropriate acknowledgement in any subsequent printing of this publication. Although we have taken all reasonable care in researching this book we make no warranty about the accuracy or completeness of its content and disclaim all liability arising from its use.

Copyright © 2016, Astute Press
All Rights Reserved.

Table of Contents

LUCCA — 6
- 🌐 GEOGRAPHY 7
- 🌐 WEATHER & BEST TIME TO VISIT 8

SIGHTS & ACTIVITIES: WHAT TO SEE & DO — 10
- 🌐 PIAZZA NAPOLEONE (PIAZZA GRANDE) 10
- 🌐 DOMUS ROMANA ARCHAEOLOGICAL SITE 11
- 🌐 CLOCK TOWER 12
- 🌐 DAY TRIP TO PISA 13
- 🌐 PIAZZA ANFITEATRO 14
- 🌐 SAN MARTINO CATHEDRAL 15
- 🌐 SAN FREDIANO CHURCH 16
- 🌐 GUINIGI TOWER 17
- 🌐 LUCCA'S CITY WALLS 18
- 🌐 SAN MICHELE CHURCH 18
- 🌐 PALAZZO PFANNER 19
- 🌐 LUCCA BOTANICAL GARDEN 21
- 🌐 PALAZZO MANSI MUSEUM 22
- 🌐 VILLA GUINIGI MUSEUM 23

BUDGET TIPS — 26
- 🌐 ACCOMMODATION 26

    La Gemma di Elena 26
    Alla Dolce Vita 27
    Leone di Sant'Anna 28
    Ostello San Frediano 28
    Casa Alba 29

🌐 RESTAURANTS, CAFÉS & BARS 30

    Ristorante Puccini 30
    Trattoria da Leo 30
    Pasticceria Taddeucci 31
    Ristorante Gli Orti di via Elisa 32
    Pizzeria Fuori di Piazza 32

🌐 SHOPPING 33

    Vissidarte 33
    Via Fillungo 34
    Enoteca Vanni 34
    Le Sorelle 35
    Benetton Stock Outlet 36

KNOW BEFORE YOU GO   37

🌐 ENTRY REQUIREMENTS 37
🌐 HEALTH INSURANCE 37
🌐 TRAVELLING WITH PETS 38
🌐 AIRPORTS 38
🌐 AIRLINES 40
🌐 CURRENCY 41
🌐 BANKING & ATMS 41
🌐 CREDIT CARDS 41
🌐 TOURIST TAXES 42
🌐 RECLAIMING VAT 42
🌐 TIPPING POLICY 43
🌐 MOBILE PHONES 43

- **DIALLING CODE** 44
- **EMERGENCY NUMBERS** 44
- **PUBLIC HOLIDAYS** 45
- **TIME ZONE** 45
- **DAYLIGHT SAVINGS TIME** 46
- **SCHOOL HOLIDAYS** 46
- **TRADING HOURS** 46
- **DRIVING LAWS** 47
- **DRINKING LAWS** 48
- **SMOKING LAWS** 48
- **ELECTRICITY** 48
- **TOURIST INFORMATION (TI)** 49
- **FOOD & DRINK** 50
- **WEBSITES** 51

LUCCA TRAVEL GUIDE

Lucca

Lucca is home to 90,000 people and is located in the scenic region of Tuscany in northwest Italy. The walled city is a treasure from medieval times that is full of 16th century charm. With beautiful well-preserved buildings, Lucca can be easily explored on foot or by bike.

LUCCA TRAVEL GUIDE

The city is rich in history dating from Ancient Roman times and has many buildings displaying their impressive Gothic architecture (from times prior to the much-discussed Renaissance era).

Lucca's walls were built to defend the city and indeed were never breached. The historical city center is located within the city walls and is home to many of the most popular sights and attractions. Lucca was also the home of Puccini, the famous Italian composer. North of Lucca are the Apuan Alps where you can visit delightful spas, mineral water springs, beautiful woods and caves.

🌍 Geography

Lucca, Tuscany is in northwest Italy, 85 kilometers west of Florence. Pisa airport is the most convenient and is situated 30 kilometers southwest of the city.

LUCCA TRAVEL GUIDE

There is a good public bus system in the Lucca area but many of the buses stop running at eight in the evening. Bus tickets can be bought from tobacco shops and you should "swipe" the ticket once on the bus. Expect to spend €1 for a single ticket. If you buy four tickets the price is reduced to €3.75.

🌍 Weather & Best Time to Visit

Lucca can get pretty hot in summertime (30C-35C highs are common), but it is mostly flat (unlike many Tuscan towns) - so you don't have to worry about walking uphill in the heat. The city walls offer some shade as well. The warmest (and busiest) months of the year are July and August and January is the coldest.

LUCCA TRAVEL GUIDE

For today's weather in Lucca see:

http://www.weather.com/weather/tenday/Lucca+Italy+ITX

X0037

LUCCA TRAVEL GUIDE

LUCCA TRAVEL GUIDE

Sights & Activities: What to See & Do

🌍 Piazza Napoleone (Piazza Grande)

55100 Lucca

Tel: +39 0583 442323

This is the largest square in Lucca and is sometimes referred to as Piazza Grande.

The square has always been the political center of the city. At the beginning of the 19th century, Lucca was held by Elisa Bonaparte Baciocchi, Napoleon's sister and she named the square after her brother. It was constructed in both the Italian and French styles. The Ducal Palace was once home to Elisa and is now the administrative building for the province of Lucca. Elisa intended to build a statue of Napoleon opposite her palace but when she lost power in 1815, the project was cancelled.

The square is one of the most peaceful areas of the city and a good place for a picnic on a warm day. During the summer, the square hosts concerts and festivals.

🌐 Domus Romana Archaeological Site

Via Cesare Battisti 15

55100 Lucca

Tel: +39 0583 050060

http://www.domusromanalucca.it/eng/domus_romana.php

This new archaeological site, located in the city center, was only discovered in 2010. The artifacts found during the excavations date from Roman times (1st century BC).

LUCCA TRAVEL GUIDE

Your guided tour to Domus Romana includes the following: taste the typical foods of the ancient Romans, watch a short documentary about the city of Lucca and the site itself (8 minutes), see a display of excavated, ancient Roman coins. You will receive a 20% discount for purchases made at the shop onsite. The entrance fee is €8. Domus Romana is open every day from 9am to 7pm.

🌐 Clock Tower ✓

Via Fillungo

55100 Lucca

Tel: +39 0583 316846

There were once 130 medieval towers located in the city of Lucca and this is the tallest that still stands. It is a fine example of beautiful medieval construction. The Clock

LUCCA TRAVEL GUIDE

Tower, otherwise known as Torre delle Ore, is located in the main street of the city center.

The tower owes its survival to the fact that it has been a public clock since 1390. Climb to the top to see stunning views of the whole city (it is the tallest building in Lucca).

The tower is open from 10:30am until 7:30pm from 1st May to 15th September.

Non-peak season opening hours are from 10:30am to 6:30pm and it is closed entirely between November and March.

The entrance costs €3.50. You can buy a joint ticket for €6.50 that covers the entrance to both the Clock Tower and the Guinigi Tower.

LUCCA TRAVEL GUIDE

🌐 Day Trip to Pisa

The nearby city of Pisa is known around the world as the location of the famous Leaning Tower of Pisa. The Leaning Tower is just one of a number of great attractions that Pisa offers. Traveling to Pisa is a typical day trip for visitors to Lucca and the two cities are only 17.5 kilometers distant.

Both cities are similar in size and population at around 90,000 each and walking is the best means of transportation as the sights are quite close to each another. Pisa has a large number of students (about two thirds of the population) and the city's university is one of the oldest in Italy. The students bring lots of culture to the city with many events, festivals, parties, concerts and more.

LUCCA TRAVEL GUIDE

Pisa is divided into four quarters. You should make it a priority to visit the Piazza dei Miracoli (Square of Miracles) which is a UNESCO World Heritage site. The sights to see in this area include the Leaning Tower of Pisa, Cathedral, Baptistry, Monumental Cemetery, and two popular art museums: the Museo del Opera del Duomo and the Museo delle Sinopie.

After you've visited the Square of Miracles visit some of the other popular sites including the Piazza dei Cavalieri and the Piazza Garibaldi. Also visit the roads along the river Arno: Lungarno Mediceo, Lungarno Pacinotti, Lungarno Galilei and Lungarno Gambacorti.

🌎 Piazza Anfiteatro

The Roman amphitheater once existed on the Piazza Anfiteatro, today's market square. Then (as today) it was the center of cultural life in Lucca and the amphitheater had a capacity of 10,000. The amphitheater was replaced by a prison, salt warehouse, and slaughterhouse (starting from medieval times). In the 19th century, the buildings were removed to use the place as a marketplace. You can still see a few remains of the Roman amphitheater however. Today, markets, festivals and fairs are held in the Piazza Anfiteatro.

🌐 San Martino Cathedral ✓

Piazza San Martino

55100 Lucca

Tel: +39 0583 957068

Visit San Martino Cathedral and take a step back to observe the architectural brilliance in front of you.

LUCCA TRAVEL GUIDE

The cathedral is constructed in a mixture of the Romanesque and Gothic styles of architecture and is located in the Piazza San Martino. The establishment was intended to be a simple church when it was constructed in the 6th century. However, two centuries later it was named as a cathedral by the pope, who consecrated it in front of 20 bishops. The cathedral underwent several periods of reconstruction. Its beauty is enhanced by the façade made in the local Lucca-Pisa style, and dates back to the 13th century (1204).

The interior was renovated in the 14th and 15th centuries, adding a touch of the then-popular Gothic style. It is rich in ancient art from the 15th and 16th centuries. The most notable artist whose work you will see is Matteo Civitali.

LUCCA TRAVEL GUIDE

If you visit during summer, it is open from 8:30am to 6pm. During the winter, the opening hours are from 9am to noon; and from 3pm to 5pm.

🌏 San Frediano Church ✓

Piazza San Frediano

55100 Lucca

Tel: + 39 0583 493627

The San Frediano church took 35 years to build at the beginning of the 12th century. There are several notable works of art, paintings and sculptures. Notice its wide façade made from white limestone with its mosaic at the top. Renovations took place across the centuries (13th / 16th / 19th century).

The church is open from 9am to noon; and from 3pm to 5pm in the summer.

During the winter, it is open from 9am to noon and from 3pm to 6pm.

🌎 Guinigi Tower ✓

Via Sant'Andrea 45

55100 Lucca

Tel: +39 0583 316846

Guinigi Tower is one of the Gothic towers still standing within the city walls of Lucca. It was built in the 14th century and remains in good condition. From the top of the tower you will notice seven trees (planted as a symbol of rebirth and power). From here there is also a breathtaking view of the city. The entrance fee to the tower is €3.50.

🌐 Lucca's City Walls ✓

Many other cities in Tuscany had their walls destroyed, but Lucca's remain to this day. Lucca's 4 km of walls have a 19th century, tree-lined pathway making a walk around them a great way to see the city. This is one of the best attractions in the city and the feature that best identifies Lucca.

🌐 San Michele Church ✓

Piazza San Michele

55100 Lucca

Tel: +39 0583 583150

This is one of the most significant buildings in the city of

LUCCA TRAVEL GUIDE

Lucca and is located in the center of the Roman Forum. It was built in the second half of the 11th century, in the Romanesque style of architecture, by request of Pope Alexander II. The façade of the church is noteable and was completed in the 13th century. It is widely known by Italians, given that it is sculpted in a rich manner. The façade was largely redone, when the San Michele church was being restored in the 19th century. Notice how the walls of the church were constructed from square white limestone blocks, typical of the Pisa and Lucca style of architecture.

Take a look at the sculpture of the Archangel Michael slaying a dragon, which serves as a crown to the church. You will see a lot of artistic beauty in the interior of the San Michele Church.

LUCCA TRAVEL GUIDE

The entrance is free of charge. Opening hours are from 9am to noon and from 3pm to 6pm during the summer. In the wintertime, it is open from 9am to noon and from 3pm to 5pm.

🌐 Palazzo Pfanner ✓

Via degli Asili 33

55100 Lucca

Tel: +39 0583 954029

http://www.palazzopfanner.it/pfanner_palace_lucca_garden_residence_museum_tours_events-1-En.html

Palazzo Pfanner is a privately owned palace that is immensely romantic. It was the setting for the 1996 movie, Portrait of a Lady, starring Nicole Kidman and John Malkovich. The palace was built in the second half of the 17th century with the gardens following in the 18th

LUCCA TRAVEL GUIDE

century. Previously owned by two other families, it was acquired by the Pfanner family in the 19th century.

Felix Pfanner was a brewer that opened the first brewery in Lucca, one of the first in Italy. The brewery was closed in 1929. The palace is still owned by the Pfanner family, who from 1995 began a detailed restoration of the Palazzo. That was also the year when they opened it up as a tourist attraction.

The complex of Palazzo Pfanner includes the building and the gardens and you pay a separate entrance fee for each attraction.

The entrance fee for the palace and garden is €4.50 each. However, there is an option for a joint ticket to both attractions, which costs €6.

LUCCA TRAVEL GUIDE

Students pay a reduced price of €4 per single entry, and €5 to visit both.

🌐 Lucca Botanical Garden ✓

Via del Giardino Botanico 14

55100 Lucca

Tel: + 39 0583 48785

The Lucca Botanical Garden was established in 1820 and one hundred years later it became the property of the city. It is situated at a corner of the city walls. The botanical garden has two sections. The first contains laboratories and greenhouses and the second section contains a pond and many trees (planted in the first half of the 19th century). Naturally, this becomes a popular attraction during the hot summer days.

LUCCA TRAVEL GUIDE

The entrance fee is €3. Students pay the reduced price of €2.

The opening hours depend on the time of the year:

from 14th Match to 30th April it is open from 10am until 5pm;

from 1st May to 30th June it is open from 10am until 6pm;

from 1st July to 18th September it is open from 10am until 7pm;

from 19th September to 16th October it is open from 10am until 5pm.

LUCCA TRAVEL GUIDE

🌐 Palazzo Mansi Museum ✓

Via Galli Tassi 43

55100 Lucca

Tel: +39 0583 55570

http://www.luccamuseinazionali.it/?l=en

This museum showcases the fortunes of the Mansi family. The palace was built at the beginning of the 17th century and purchased by Ascanio Mansi in 1916. At the end of the 17th century the palace was renovated and during the next century it became the center of society life. Ten years after his death (in 1956), his sons sold the palace to the state of Lucca.

The entrance to the Palazzo Mansi Museum is €4. Under 18's and over-65's are free of charge. Students pay €2.

LUCCA TRAVEL GUIDE

Opening hours are from 8:30am to 7:30pm and the museum is open every day, except Sunday.

🌐 Villa Guinigi Museum ✓

Via della Quarquonia

55100 Lucca

Tel: +39 0583 496033

http://www.luccamuseinazionali.it/?l=en

This museum is located in one of the oldest and most luxurious palaces in Lucca. The palace was built in the 15th century and was as a pleasure palace for the ruler of Lucca, Paolo Guinigi.

Early in the 20th century, the palace was converted into a museum and underwent several restorations in order for it to be taken back to its previous beauty. Nowadays, the

LUCCA TRAVEL GUIDE

Villa Guinigi Museum houses five exhibitions which show five eras of the city, starting with the Ancient Roman.

The entrance to the museum costs €4. Everyone under the age of 18 and over the age of 65 can enter free of charge. Students pay the reduced price of €2. There is also an option of buying a joint ticket for both the Palazzo Mansi Museum and the Villa Guinigi Museum for €6.50, with students paying the reduced price of €3.25.

The museum is open every day, except Sunday, from 8:30am to 7:30pm.

LUCCA TRAVEL GUIDE

Budget Tips

🌐 Accommodation

La Gemma di Elena

Via della Zecca 33

55100 Lucca

Tel: +39 0583 496665

http://www.lagemmadielena.it/en/

This is a perfect choice if you are looking for a nice place to stay but don't want to spend a lot of money. La Gemma di Elena is located in the historical center of Lucca, the oldest part of the city and within the walls. Thanks to the location of this bed & breakfast, you can reach most of the city attractions in no time. You will still enjoy all the peace and quiet you need.

LUCCA TRAVEL GUIDE

There is a friendly environment in this bed & breakfast and breakfast is included in the price of your stay. The most inexpensive rooms do not have a private bathroom. The price for a single room with a shared bathroom is €35; while the double will set you back €50 (€65 if you want a private bathroom).

Alla Dolce Vita

Via Fillungo 232

55100 Lucca

Tel: +39 3295 825062

http://www.luccabed.com/

Alla Dolce Vita is perfect for visitors who want to be located close to the main city attractions, without having to spend a lot of money on accommodation. The guesthouse is located in the historical center of Lucca.

LUCCA TRAVEL GUIDE

Alla Dolce Vita was built in the 19th century and has been thoroughly renovated. It holds the charm of its old architectural style. All rooms include a private bathroom. A double room will set you back anywhere from €45-67, depending on the season. The price for a triple room is from €54-77.

Leone di Sant'Anna

Via Castruccio Buonamici 221

55100 Lucca

Tel: +39 0583 1680929

http://www.leonedisantanna.com/en/

This bed & breakfast is located in the center of the city, making it easy for you to visit some of the most popular tourist attractions in Lucca. Leone di Sant'Anna has a friendly environment and a staff that will help with any

LUCCA TRAVEL GUIDE

type of tourist information you need. The ambience is relaxing. A double room in this bed & breakfast will set you back around €70-80.

Ostello San Frediano

Via della Cavallerizza 12

55100 Lucca

Tel: +39 0583 469957

http://www.ostellolucca.it/hostel/index.asp

Backpackers, this is the place for you! This hostel will provide you with the opportunity to meet many passionate travelers like yourself. It is located next to the famous walls of Lucca, in the historical center of the city. It is perfect if you plan on visiting the most famous attractions on foot. When you return to the hostel you can enjoy a book or magazine from their library. Wi-Fi is also included in the price of your stay. You will spend €20 for a dorm bed in a room that holds 6 to 8 people.

Casa Alba

Via Fillungo 142

55100 Lucca

Tel: +39 3355 720642

http://www.casa-alba.com/en/index.php

This is a great bed & breakfast, located inside the walls of Lucca. Each room has a private bathroom. Wi-Fi and a continental breakfast are included in the price of your stay. Expect to spend around €55-78 for a double room per night. A single room costs about €40-60 per night, depending on the season.

LUCCA TRAVEL GUIDE

🌐 Restaurants, Cafés & Bars

Ristorante Puccini

Corte San Lorenzo 1

55100 Lucca

Tel: +39 3389 805927

This restaurant is located in the historical center of Lucca. Despite its great location, it is not an expensive place to eat. This is a family restaurant with great hospitality. The family that owns the Ristorante Puccini are friendly to visitors, and will make sure that you are provided with top quality Italian food.

Trattoria da Leo

Via Tegrimi 1

55100 Lucca

LUCCA TRAVEL GUIDE

Tel: +39 0583 492236

http://www.trattoriadaleo.it/Home_en.html

The most authentic restaurants in Italy are family owned, just like Trattoria da Leo. This is a traditional and relaxing restaurant offering nice, cheap Italian food.

It is open from noon to 2:30pm; and from 7:30pm to 10:30pm. Expect to spend around €7 for one of their great dishes.

Pasticceria Taddeucci

Piazza San Michele 34

55100 Lucca

Tel: +39 0583 494933

The best food you will eat in Lucca will not necessarily be

from a restaurant. This bakery is sure to keep you coming back for more. Don't miss the buccellato, their famous sweet bread with raisins. It is available in different sizes (300/600/900g) and will cost about €4/8/12, depending on the size of the loaf. Pasticceria Taddeucci was built in the second half of the 19th century, and it still holds that old and traditional ambience. The bakery is open from 8:30am to 7:45pm.

Ristorante Gli Orti di via Elisa

Via Elisa 17

55100 Lucca

Tel: +39 0583 491241

http://www.ristorantegliorti.it/LENG/Z2/C9616-0/hhcm-Home.html

This restaurant is immensely popular among locals. It is

LUCCA TRAVEL GUIDE

located in the historical center of the city, and is done in traditional style. The cooking methods are traditional Italian. The menu offers top quality of local cuisine. Once you take the first bite, you will realize why it is constantly packed. Reservations are advisable.

Pizzeria Fuori di Piazza

Piazza Napoleone 16

55100 Lucca

Tel: +39 0583 491322

This restaurant is a great choice if you want to eat traditional local pizza. Pizza here is prepared as a simple dish, without too many extra ingredients. That's the best way.

🌐 Shopping

Vissidarte

Via Calderia 20

55100 Lucca

Tel: +39 0583 48383

Want a long-lasting item that will always remind you of your trip to Lucca? This shop sells top quality ceramics using designs that are traditional for this part of Tuscany. The owner is just as pleasant as the items he sells. He will gladly explain the history behind each of the ceramic items. This shop is even open on Sundays, unlike most stores in Italy.

LUCCA TRAVEL GUIDE

Via Fillungo

55100 Lucca

There is no better place to shop than on the main shopping street in the city. On Via Fillungo there are many shops selling souvenirs, international designer clothes, local clothing items, and more. This is a traditional street with a lot of old buildings to look at along the way. After some shopping you can enjoy a break at one of the cafés and restaurants. Keep in mind that most of the shops on this street are closed on Mondays.

Enoteca Vanni

Piazza San Salvatore 7

55100 Lucca

Tel: +39 0583 491902

http://www.enotecavanni.com/enoteca-vanni-en.asp

LUCCA TRAVEL GUIDE

Italians love drinking a glass of wine while enjoying a meal. During your visit you should taste as many different types of wine as possible. To actually learn about the wines, visit Enoteca Vanni where you can taste and buy some of the finest wines in Tuscany. It was opened in 1965, and since then has supplied locals and foreigners with top quality wines. Enoteca Vanni is located in the historical center of Lucca; so while you are out visiting some of the attractions in the city, be sure to visit this shop. They offer a great selection of wines, liquors, olive oil and typical local food.

Le Sorelle

Piazza Anfiteatro 31

55100 Lucca

Tel: +39 0583 48631

LUCCA TRAVEL GUIDE

This is a great place to buy a souvenir for yourself and gifts for your friends and family. You can choose from a lot of handmade products. The soaps are recommended as is their olive oil. The shop is located in the Roman Amphitheater section of the city.

Benetton Stock Outlet

Via Mordini 17/19

55100 Lucca

Tel: +39 0583 464533

The Benetton Stock Outlet is a great place to spend a little money for a high quality product. They offer a great selection of clothing items for both men and women. This is the perfect place if you want to leave with lots of

LUCCA TRAVEL GUIDE

shopping bags while still having some money in your purse or wallet!

LUCCA TRAVEL GUIDE

Know Before You Go

🌐 Entry Requirements

By virtue of the Schengen agreement, travellers from other countries in the European Union do not need a visa when visiting Italy. Additionally Swiss travellers are also exempt. Visitors from certain other countries such as the USA, Canada, Japan, Israel, Australia and New Zealand do not need visas if their stay in Italy does not exceed 90 days. When entering Italy you will be required to make a declaration of presence, either at the airport, or at a police station within eight days of arrival. This applies to visitors from other Schengen countries, as well as those visiting from non-Schengen countries.

🌐 Health Insurance

Citizens of other EU countries are covered for emergency health care in Italy. UK residents, as well as visitors from Switzerland are covered by the European Health Insurance Card (EHIC), which can be applied for free of charge. Visitors from non-Schengen countries will need to show proof of private health insurance that is valid for the duration of their stay in

Italy (that offers at least €37,500 coverage), as part of their visa application. No special vaccinations are required.

🌐 Travelling with Pets

Italy participates in the Pet Travel Scheme (PETS) which allows UK residents to travel with their pets without requiring quarantine upon re-entry. Certain conditions will need to be met. The animal will have to be microchipped and up to date on rabies vaccinations. In the case of dogs, a vaccination against canine distemper is also required by the Italian authorities. When travelling from the USA, your pet will need to be microchipped or marked with an identifying tattoo and up to date on rabies vaccinations. An EU Annex IV Veterinary Certificate for Italy will need to be issued by an accredited veterinarian. On arrival in Italy, you can apply for an EU pet passport to ease your travel in other EU countries.

🌐 Airports

Fiumicino – Leonardo da Vinci International Airport (FCO) is one of the busiest airports in Europe and the main international airport of Italy. It is located about 35km southwest of the historical quarter of Rome. Terminal 5 is used for trans-Atlantic and international flights, while Terminals 1, 2 and 3 serve mainly for domestic flights and medium haul flights to other European destinations. Before Leonardo da Vinci replaced it, the **Ciampino–G. B. Pastine International Airport** (CIA) was the main international airport servicing Rome and Italy. It is one of the oldest airports in the country still in use. Although it declined in importance, budget airlines such as Ryanair boosted its air traffic in recent years. The airport is used by Wizz Air, V Bird, Helvetic, Transavia Airlines, Sterling, Ryanair, Thomsonfly, EasyJet, Air Berlin, Hapag-Lloyd Express and Carpatair.

Milan Malpensa Airport (MXP) is the largest of the three airports serving the city of Milan. Located about 40km northwest of Milan's city center, it connects travellers to the regions of Lombardy, Piedmont and Liguria. **Milan Linate Airport** (LIN) is Milan's second international airport. **Venice Marco Polo Airport** (VCE) provides access to the charms of Venice. **Olbia Costa Smeralda Airport** (OLB) is located near Olbia, Sardinia. Main regional airports are **Guglielmo Marconi Airport** (BLQ), an international airport servicing the region of Bologna, **Capodichino Airport** at Naples (NAP), **Pisa International Airport** (PSA), formerly Galileo Galilei Airport, the main airport serving Tuscany, **Sandro Pertini Airport** near Turin (TRN), **Cristoforo Colombo** in Genoa (GOA), **Punta Raisi Airport** in Palermo (PMO), **Vincenzo Bellini Airport** in Catania (CTA) and **Palese Airport** in Bari (BRI).

LUCCA TRAVEL GUIDE

🌐 Airlines

Alitalia is the flag carrier and national airline of Italy. It has a subsidiary, Alitalia CityLiner, which operates short-haul regional flights. Air Dolomiti is a regional Italian based subsidiary of of the Lufthansa Group. Meridiana is a privately owned airline based at Olbia in Sardinia.

Fiumicino - Leonardo da Vinci International Airport serves as the main hub for Alitalia, which has secondary hubs at Milan Linate and Milan Malpensa Airport. Alitalia CityLiner uses Fiumicino – Leonardo da Vinci International Airport as main hub and has secondary hubs at Milan-Linate, Naples and Trieste. Fiumicino – Leonardo da Vinci International Airport is also one of two primary hubs used by the budget Spanish airline Vueling. Milan Malpensa Airport is one of the largest bases for the British budget airline EasyJet. Venice Airport serves as an Italian base for the Spanish budget airline, Volotea, which provides connections mainly to other destinations in Europe. Olbia Costa Smeralda Airport (OLB), located near Olbia, Sardinia is the primary base of Meridiana, a private Italian Airline in partnership with Air Italia and Fly Egypt.

🌐 Currency

Italy's currency is the Euro. It is issued in notes in denominations of €500, €200, €100, €50, €20, €10 and €5.

LUCCA TRAVEL GUIDE

Coins are issued in denominations of €2, €1, 50c, 20c, 10c, 5c, 2c and 1c.

🌐 Banking & ATMs

Using ATMs or Bancomats, as they are known in Italy, to withdraw money is simple if your ATM card is compatible with the MasterCard/Cirrus or Visa/Plus networks. There is a €250 limit on daily withdrawals. Italian machines are configured for 4-digit PIN numbers, although some machines will be able to handle longer PIN numbers. Bear in mind some Bancomats can run out of cash over weekends and that the more remote villages may not have adequate banking facilities so plan ahead.

🌐 Credit Cards

Credit cards are valid tender in most Italian businesses. While Visa and MasterCard are accepted universally, most tourist oriented businesses also accept American Express and Diners Club. Credit cards issued in Europe are smart cards that that are fitted with a microchip and require a PIN for each transaction. This means that a few ticket machines, self-service vendors and other businesses may not be configured to accept the older magnetic strip credit cards. Do remember to advise your bank or credit card company of your travel plans before leaving.

LUCCA TRAVEL GUIDE

🌐 Tourist Taxes

Tourist tax varies from city to city, as each municipality sets its own rate. The money is collected by your accommodation and depends on the standard of accommodation. A five star establishment will levy a higher amount than a four star or three star establishment. You can expect to pay somewhere between €1 and €7 per night, with popular destinations like Rome, Venice, Milan and Florence charging a higher overall rate. In some regions, the rate is also adjusted seasonally. Children are usually exempt until at least the age of 10 and sometimes up to the age of 18. In certain areas, disabled persons and their companions also qualify for discounted rates. Tourist tax is payable directly to the hotel or guesthouse before the end of your stay.

🌐 Reclaiming VAT

If you are not from the European Union, you can claim back VAT (Value Added Tax) paid on your purchases in Italy. The VAT rate in Italy is 21 percent and this can be claimed back on your purchases if certain conditions are met. The merchant needs to be partnered with a VAT refund program. This will be indicated if the shop displays a "Tax Free" sign. The shop assistant will fill out a form for reclaiming VAT. When you submit this at the airport, you will receive your refund.

LUCCA TRAVEL GUIDE

🌐 Tipping Policy

If your bill includes the phrase "coperto e servizio", that means that a service charge or tip is already included. Most waiting staff in Italy are salaried workers, but if the service is excellent, a few euros extra would be appreciated.

🌐 Mobile Phones

Most EU countries, including Italy use the GSM mobile service. This means that most UK phones and some US and Canadian phones and mobile devices will work in Italy. While you could check with your service provider about coverage before you leave, using your own service in roaming mode will involve additional costs. The alternative is to purchase an Italian SIM card to use during your stay in Italy.

Italy has four mobile networks. They are TIM, Wind, Vodafone and Tre (3) and they all provide pre-paid services. TIM offers two tourist options, both priced at €20 (+ €10 for the SIM card) with a choice of two packages - 2Gb data, plus 200 minutes call time or internet access only with a data allowance of 5Gb. Vodafone, Italy's second largest network offers a Vodafone Holiday package including SIM card for €30. They also offer the cheapest roaming rates. Wind offers an Italian Tourist pass for €20 which includes 100 minutes call time and 2Gb data and can be extended with a restart option for an extra €10.

LUCCA TRAVEL GUIDE

To purchase a local SIM card, you will need to show your passport or some other form of identification and provide your residential details in Italy. By law, SIM registration is required prior to activation. Most Italian SIM cards expire after a 90 day period of inactivity. When dialling internationally, remember to use the (+) sign and the code of the country you are connecting to.

🌐 Dialling Code

The international dialling code for Italy is +39.

🌐 Emergency Numbers

Police: 113

Fire: 115

Ambulance: 118

MasterCard: 800 789 525

Visa: 800 819 014

🌐 Public Holidays

1 January: New Year's Day (Capodanno)

6 January: Day of the Epiphany (Epifania)

March-April: Easter Monday (Lunedì dell'Angelo or Pasquetta)

25 April: Liberation Day (Festa della Liberazione)

1 May: International Worker's Day (Festa del Lavoro / Festa dei Lavoratori)

2 June: Republic Day (Festa della Repubblica)

15 August: Assumption Day (Ferragosto / Assunta)

1 November: All Saints Day (Tutti i santi / Ognissanti)

8 December: Immaculate Conception (Immacolata Concezione / Immacolata)

25 December: Christmas Day (Natale)

26 December: St Stephen's Day (Santo Stefano)

A number of Saints days are observed regionally throughout the year.

🌍 Time Zone

Italy falls in the Central European Time Zone. This can be calculated as Greenwich Mean Time/Coordinated Universal Time (GMT/UTC) +2; Eastern Standard Time (North America) -6; Pacific Standard Time (North America) -9.

🌍 Daylight Savings Time

Clocks are set forward one hour on 29 March and set back one hour on 25 October for Daylight Savings Time.

LUCCA TRAVEL GUIDE

🌐 School Holidays

The academic year begins in mid September and ends in mid June. The summer holiday is from mid June to mid September, although the exact times may vary according to region. There are short breaks around Christmas and New Year and also during Easter. Some regions such as Venice and Trentino have an additional break during February for the carnival season.

🌐 Trading Hours

Trading hours for the majority of shops are from 9am to 12.30pm and then again from 3.30pm to 7.30pm, although in some areas, the second shift may be from 4pm to 8pm instead. The period between 1pm and 4pm is known in Italy as the *riposo*. Large department shops and malls tend to be open from 9am to 9pm, from Monday to Saturday. Post offices are open from 8.30am to 1.30pm from Monday to Saturday. Most shops and many restaurants are closed on Sundays. Banking hours are from 8.30am to 1.30pm and then again from 3pm to 4pm, Monday to Friday. Most restaurants are open from noon till 2.30pm and then again from 7pm till 11pm or midnight, depending on the establishment. Nightclubs open around 10pm, but only liven up after midnight. Closing times vary, but will generally be between 2am and 4am. Museum hours vary,

LUCCA TRAVEL GUIDE

although major sights tend to be open continuously and often up to 7.30pm. Many museums are closed on Mondays.

🌍 Driving Laws

The Italians drive on the right hand side of the road. A driver's licence from any of the European Union member countries is valid in Italy. Visitors from non-EU countries will require an International Driving Permit that must remain current throughout the duration of their stay in Italy.

The speed limit on Italy's autostrade is 130km per hour and 110km per hour on main extra-urban roads, but this is reduced by 20km to 110km and 90km respectively in rainy weather. On secondary extra-urban roads, the speed limit is 90km per hour; on urban highways, it is 70km per hour and on urban roads, the speed limit is 50km per hour. You are not allowed to drive in the ZTL or Limited Traffic Zone (or *zona traffico limitato* in Italian) unless you have a special permit.

Visitors to Italy are allowed to drive their own non-Italian vehicles in the country for a period of up to six months. After this, they will be required to obtain Italian registration with Italian licence plates. Italy has very strict laws against driving under the influence of alcohol. The blood alcohol limit is 0.05 and drivers caught above the limit face penalties such as fines of up to €6000, confiscation of their vehicles, suspension of their licenses and imprisonment of up to 6 months. Breathalyzer tests are routine at accident scenes.

🌐 Drinking Laws

The legal drinking age in Italy is 16. While drinking in public spaces is allowed, public drunkenness is not tolerated. Alcohol is sold in bars, wine shops, liquor stores and grocery shops.

🌐 Smoking Laws

In 2005, Italy implemented a policy banning smoking from public places such as bars, restaurants, nightclubs and working places, limiting it to specially designated smoking rooms. Further legislation banning smoking from parks, beaches and stadiums is being explored.

🌐 Electricity

Electricity: 220 volts

Frequency: 50 Hz

Italian electricity sockets are compatible with the Type L plugs, a plug that features three round pins or prongs, arranged in a straight line. An alternate is the two-pronged Type C Euro adaptor. If travelling from the USA, you will need a power converter or transformer to convert the voltage from 220 to 110, to avoid damage to your appliances. The latest models of many laptops, camcorders, mobile phones and digital cameras are dual-voltage with a built in converter.

🌎 Tourist Information (TI)

There are tourist information (TI) desks at each of the terminals of the Leonardo da Vinci International Airport, as well as interactive Information kiosks with the latest touch-screen technology. In Rome, the tourist office can be found at 5 Via Parigi, near the Termini Station and it is identified as APT, which stands for Azienda provinciale del Turismo. Free maps and brochures of current events are available from tourist kiosks.

Several of the more tourist-oriented regions of Italy offer tourist cards that include admission to most of the city's attractions. While these cards are not free, some offer great value for money. A variety of tourism apps are also available online.

🌎 Food & Drink

Pasta is a central element of many typically Italian dishes, but there are regional varieties and different types of pasta are matched to different sauces. Well known pasta dishes such as lasagne and bolognaise originated in Bologna. Stuffed pasta is popular in the northern part of Italy, while the abundance of seafood and olives influences southern Italian cuisine. As far as pizza goes, the Italians differentiate between the thicker Neapolitan pizza and the thin crust Roman pizza, as well as white pizza, also known as focaccia and tomato based pizza. Other standards include minestrone soup, risotto, polenta and a variety of cheeses, hams, sausages and salamis. If you are on a budget, consider snacking on stuzzichini with a few drinks during happy hour which is often between 7 and 9pm. The fare can include salami, cheeses, cured meat, mini pizzas, bread, vegetables, pastries or pate. In Italy, Parmesan refers only to cheese originating from the area surrounding Parma. Favorites desserts include tiramisu or Italian gelato.

Italians enjoy relaxing to aperitifs before they settle down to a meal and their favorites are Campari, Aperol or Negroni, the famous Italian cocktail. Wine is enjoyed with dinner. Italy is particularly famous for its red wines. The best known wine regions are Piedmont, which produces robust and dry reds, Tuscany and Alto Adige, where Alpine soil adds a distinctive acidity. After the meal, they settle down to a glass of limoncello, the country's most popular liqueur, or grappa, which is distilled from grape seeds and stems, as digestive. Other options in this class include a nut liqueur, nocino, strawberry based Fragolino Veneto or herbal digestives like gineprino, laurino or mirto. Italians are also fond of coffee. Espresso is drunk through throughout the day, but cappuccino is considered a morning drink. The most popular beers in Italy are Peroni and Moretti.

🌐 Websites

http://vistoperitalia.esteri.it/home/en

This is the website of the Consulate General of Italy. Here you can look up whether you will need a visa and also process your application online.

http://www.italia.it/en/home.html

The official website of Italian tourism

http://www.italia.it/en/useful-info/mobile-apps.html

Select the region of your choice to download a useful mobile app to your phone.

http://www.italylogue.com/tourism

http://italiantourism.com/index.html

http://www.reidsitaly.com/

http://wikitravel.org/en/Italy

https://www.summerinitaly.com/

http://www.accessibleitalianholiday.com/

Planning Italian vacations around the needs of disabled tourists.

Printed in Great Britain
by Amazon